DIANA WINTERFELD

THE PAIN BEHIND HER SMILE

(Surviving PTSD)

DEDICATION

To God, who gave me the gift and vision to write this book. And the courage and strength to press forward.

"The Lord will fight for you, you need only to be still."

~ Exodus 14:14

Contents

ACKNOWLEDGMENTS

This book is dedicated to my three beautiful children, from whom I constantly drew strength to go on. To my mom, who taught me the foundation of faith. Without faith, I would not be here today. And to my incredible husband, Steve, who has shown me what true love looks like. His unconditional love and support have blessed me in so many ways. I have waited a lifetime to meet my soulmate, and it has been worth the wait.

Thank you, God for putting them all around me through one of my toughest journeys in my life, surviving PTSD. Yes, SURVIVING Post Traumatic Stress Disorder.

God is by my side, with the Holy Spirit as my co-author. I have learned to keep God right by me, to guide me and give me strength to relive the past through my writing.

It's time to rethink memories that I have tucked away safely, in order to heal and put them behind me.

These feelings that I have, my heart racing, tension in my jaws and tears rolling down my face, surprise me. I have put the work in of healing and becoming victorious from the past abuse. But my story needs to be told. We are all given testimony throughout our lives to help impact others as they go through their tough times. The dark times that bring you back through to the light as a stronger and more enlightened person.

I know how many books have made a real impact on my own life, and my prayer is that this book will do that for you as well. It has made an impact on my own life; it has helped me learn and grow through my writing.

As I prayed for guidance, I not only received guidance but also teaching from the Holy Spirit. Life-changing teaching. Because of it, my life has changed entirely for the better.

My goal is to have this book published as a way for me to widen my comfort zone and have a higher purpose. To also give others hope to hang on and to move forward. To not stay a victim, but be victorious.

Chapter One
DEVELOPING A PASSIVE CHILD

I was a small-town girl who was the easy-going, happy-go-lucky girl that wanted to be a friend to everyone. The high school cheerleader, dating the football player. After all, that's the ultimate high school dream, right? Everyone thought we were the perfect couple. But this "easy-going girl" was really just a passive people-pleaser, walking into a future of not standing up for myself, but devaluing myself enough to not be treated the way I deserved to be treated. Before I ever met him, I was already losing my value through ongoing circumstances as a child.

I was raised to learn how to be passive, out of what was viewed as being respectful to my parents. Children were to be seen and not heard. If we stood up for ourselves or disagreed with what was being said, it was considered talking back. We were not to talk back and just do as we were told. With this rule in place, how were we to learn to assert ourselves with other people when things were not right in our eyes and in our hearts? When our feelings are hurt by another person's actions, shouldn't we tell them we have been hurt by them, regardless of their age?

Does being "seen and not heard" teach us to assert ourselves? Does it prepare us for good communication with our peers when we are growing up? No, it does not. It creates passive children like I was.

Yes, we can be respectful children, yet be given a safe place by our parents to be able to speak up when our feelings have been hurt in a situation that doesn't feel right to us. I learned to stuff my feelings away at a very young age. I do not hold that against my parents because I know they were doing things the way they were taught.

The "seen and not heard" rule I was raised with is a "core belief" that I now understand can send your children out into the world without the good communication skills they need. The skills that will help them assert themselves. This will help them not to allow themselves to be walked all over by others, even bullied, like I was.

My mom was a single mom raising four children, all within a year of each other. Because healthy communication was not learned in our home, we grew up internalizing everything. We did not lean on one another to help get through tough situations in our lives. Life was basically growing up through trial and error. Thank goodness for the foundation of having God in our home. With this foundation in place, it allowed me to not steer too far off the right path, for too long. Though because of my passive nature, I did become a follower and a crowd pleaser for most of my twenties. During this time frame, I stopped keeping God as my center. My soul became very lost being someone that wasn't leading, but only following. I was helping no one, not even myself.

My learned behavior was: if your feelings had been hurt by your parents, let it go as quickly as possible. Do not talk about it out of respect for your parents. Therefore, I was raised a passive child who, when things didn't feel right, became an overachiever at being silent and well-behaved. I learned how to be a person who always wanted to keep the peace and not cause any waves in my home or with my peers. I worked very faithfully at being a people-pleaser.

I was also raised thinking that if people did not think the way I did, they were wrong, and I was right. It was another core belief that, as an adult, I realized I would need to work through and respect people's opinions and perspectives.

I had been rejecting them instead of realizing that God makes us all unique for His higher purpose. People have different perspectives because of their own personal experiences.

We don't have to agree with them but respect their own perspectives. People should not be made to feel insignificant because they think differently than we do. Nor should we try to force them to think like we do. My core belief growing up was that if people didn't think like I did about life, then their thinking was wrong. It has taken me a long time to retrain my thinking and to accept everyone as individuals on their own personal journeys.

All I should be doing is living my life as an example to all, with God's guidance. It is where my focus should be. I should also focus on loving all and accepting them where they are at in life, while praying for them. That is how I would like the people around me to treat me as well. Love one another and pray for each other. No one knows or understands your journey but God.

Meet them where they are at and treat them the way you would want to be treated. Treat them with love and kindness.

> **"The Lord is near the brokenhearted and saves the crushed in spirit." ~Psalms 34:18**

Prayer: *Lord, thank you for watching over me and hearing what was only to stay in my heart and not come out as spoken words. You are healing the wounds created through my silence, and love me through my past pain. ~Amen~*

Chapter Two
DATING "PRINCE CHARMING."

I stumbled into a date with "Prince Charming", the popular football player that had a lot of people's attention, some good attention and some not so good attention. I had been with a friend who had jokingly suggested "Prince Charming" take me to a barbecue that was going to take place in a few days at a friend's home. It was to take place in our small hometown in Idaho, after a high school football game. We all jokingly laughed off the suggestion of us going there together. However, "Prince Charming" took it as a set plan. I did not want to hurt his feelings, and quickly put his feelings over mine and allowed the date to take place. This mistake was something that I would master throughout my relationship with him.

"Prince Charming" had his full charm in action, and it turned out to be the best date I had ever been on. Not that I had been on many dates as a young, naïve sixteen-year-old girl. He basically treated me like a Princess. I was off on a thirty-year adventure that would bring me to where I am today, writing this book to tell my story.

"Prince Charming" was not who he appeared to be when we were around others. Behind closed doors, I was constantly excusing away bad and abusive behavior and accepting it because of his own abusive childhood.

When I started dating him, I soon realized he was not living with his mom, but with another family. I only saw things from how they were in my home, which was a safe environment, with my single mom raising four children in a God-fearing home. So with that being said, I had no idea encouraging him to go back and live with his mom would actually be putting him back into an unsafe and emotionally abusive environment. He basically went back into the Lion's Den filled with more emotional and physical abuse, which I would eventually be treated the same way by him, and worse. "The abused become the abuser."

Just like my future relationship would be with him, his relationship with his mom would have good times that would eventually be washed out with angry, hurtful words towards him, even anger directed towards me within time. She would walk into the house almost nightly drunk and angry. There were mean hurtful things spewed toward him, as he sat in silence. I even watched her hitting on him with her fists one night, as he put up his arms up in defense. I was shocked and deeply saddened that the one person in his life that should be protecting him, was so cruel.

I quickly developed a protective relationship toward him. When he took his anger out on me, I dismissed it because I understood why he was angry and who he was really angry with. I continued to put his feelings over mine, as our own abuse cycle was developing and continued to increase as time progressed.

Later in life, once I left the abuse cycle, I was told that though I understood why the abuse was happening in my relationship with him, I didn't have to accept it. Accepting it would allow it to continue with unhealthy boundaries set and an abusive relationship that would grow into a relationship from hell. Hell, I almost didn't survive.

I was sixteen years old when I was first abused physically by "Prince Charming". I had never stood up for myself. Without that first time being dealt with emotionally, I never healed. I just dismissed it, excused it off and buried it deep inside.

> **"Love is patient, love is kind. It does not dishonor others." ~1 Corinthians 13:4-5**

Prayer: *God, please heal me from the past, when I did not know what true love was. Thank you for showing me your love and bringing true love to me.*

~Amen~

Chapter Three
MEETING SYBIL

By telling my story, my prayer is to be able to reach others by raising awareness of unhealthy learned behaviors. If I can change and learn healthier boundaries, anyone can. After all, by the time I walked into my therapist's office for the first time, I was, as she called it, "in my eleventh hour". She told me once I was stable that she truly didn't believe I was ever coming back. I had stayed in the relationship of abuse for so long that it had broken me into a million emotional pieces, shattered beyond repair, or so we all thought.

God guides me and teaches me daily to assert myself in a healthier manner. I have learned to express what I am feeling more openly to people and not keep it tucked away safely inside of me. Because it truly is not safe, but in fact very destructive. I have learned to stand up for myself and the people around me.

Sadly at first, the assertion came out in a very unhealthy manner, through another personality I had been totally unaware even existed. She was a person who was nothing like the passive girl I had grown up to be.

Once I realized that it was a part of me, I quickly gave this personality her own name, which was Sybil.

During the abuse cycle, my second personality was being developed deep down inside of me. She wasn't allowed to come out and protect me though. It was not a safe place for either of us to be.

She did not show herself until it was safe. Once I got away from "Prince Charming", this other personality came to the surface. She came out when she felt she needed to protect me from someone. She would step up and "protect" Diana. She wasn't going to let anyone ever hurt us again.

Sybil was a part of me that became an aggressive sixteen-year-old personality that came out when, as an adult, I was feeling threatened. Maybe if she could have dealt with those emotions when the abuse first started when I was a child, this story would be a completely different one to tell.

She was a very strong, angry, and aggressive girl. Everything she should have been when I was in fact sixteen years old. She was a side of me I had never shown. This sixteen-year-old girl, who should have stood up for herself, even in her own home, had stayed deep down inside of me. Sybil began to develop the very first time I was abused by "Prince Charming" at the young age of sixteen. I had been handing my feelings to her, to safely tuck away.

When I started dating "Prince Charming," it was the first time I experienced physical abuse from a boyfriend. I was grabbed and thrown over a trash can when I tried to break up with him. And so the cycle of abuse began. His manipulative, sorrowful tears would soon be followed by anger, quickly throwing us back into the "honeymoon phase" of our relationship. After all, I was a Christian girl with a lot of love and compassion.

Once again, out of guilt from the unacceptable behavior, I would be treated like a Princess. Love bombing would start again. I had a kind and forgiving heart, and believed each time he was truly sorry and it would never happen again. I was constantly making up new excuses for his behavior. I protected him by never telling anyone what was happening. I could handle this. I was a strong girl, and I could love his anger and the hurt away.

This cycle went on for years, sometimes with very little honeymoon in between. The happy times started to never come. I believe the honeymoon part of the cycle was not lasting as long because I no longer was falling for the "Prince Charming" treatment. I started to spend my time waiting for the next time that I would be a victim to his anger, and never could let my guard down. This created more anger and frustration in him, and the aggression came more frequently.

He was constantly harassing me about how I was treating him. He was very good at victimizing himself, so that he wouldn't need to take responsibility for his bad behavior. There would never be a true apology.

He told me I chose to be sad, and that there was nothing he could do to ever please me. I was held accountable for my feelings towards him, instead of him taking any responsibility for any of the problems between us. I was even told by his best friend that the problems in the relationship were my fault, because I wasn't being submissive to "Prince Charming".

Submitting to him at that point would have been allowing him to abuse our children without me doing what I could to protect them. It was so frustrating and painful to be judged by someone who had no idea what was happening behind closed doors. The mama bear wasn't going anywhere.

The phrase "You need help, Diana" was one of his constant war cries. He even went as far as to drive me to an Urgent Care and demand that I go in and seek help for my depression.

My spirit continued to be broken as I isolated myself from family and friends. It became too hard for me to smile and be the person that people knew me to be.

> **"I waited patiently for the Lord; he turned to me and heard my cry. He lifted me out of the slimy pit, out of the mud and mire; he set my feet on a rock and gave me a firm place to stand." ~Psalms 40:1-2**

Prayer: *God, I know through the valleys, your hand is molding and shaping me, for my story to be told, through your eyes, and led by your thoughts and teachings. Thank you for watching over me as I tell my story.*

~Amen~

Chapter Four
A TRUE PASSIVE FRIEND

I was a good friend to have around for some people. They could walk all over me and behave the way they wanted because I would not hold them accountable for my hurt feelings and mistreatment. I would smile and laugh away the hurt, as I had masterfully learned to do. Quickly tucking those hurt feelings away and continuing on with the unhealthy relationships. I was very good at building those friends up and making them feel good. If I quickly tucked away my hurt feelings safely, then it would be okay.

If I ever stood up for myself, it usually went very badly. I was talked over, belittled, and went unheard. I walked away from the situation, even less empowered, and was made to feel responsible for saying anything that reflected poorly on them.

I was the perfect friend for a narcissist.

> **"Above all guard your heart, for everything you do flows from it." ~Proverbs 4:23**

Prayer: *God, thank you for being my Father and teaching me throughout my journey about self-love.*

~Amen~

Chapter Five
THE ASSERTIVE NEW ME

When I started my journey of learning to be strong and assert myself, I soon realized there were people around me that were passive-aggressive. Not a few of them, but a lot of them. They would need to be kept at a distance and not be part of my inner circle of family and friends.

I stood up for myself with a family member, and the table was quickly turned back towards me so that the situation would not reflect badly on them. I was asked, "What is wrong with you? Are you pre-menopausal?" It occurred to me then, that there are certain people in my life who will not take constructive criticism and learn from it, or even apologize for their wrong behavior. With these types of people, I would need to limit my time with them in order to have my own healthy boundaries.

If I could say anything to them that would allow a healthier relationship with them, I would have done so. Only God could change their behavior. Only God could change their hardened hearts. I would be praying for them instead.

I needed to step back and protect my own heart from unhealthy relationships around me. Once I started doing this, I realized that it was going to be protecting myself from most of the people in my inner circle.

I soon started losing friends, as I began to start taking care of my own heart, and setting healthier boundaries for myself.

I spent a lot of time grieving because of the losses. Most of the people in my inner circle were Passive Aggressive Narcissists. As I asserted myself with them, they quickly turned the tables and made me accountable for the relationship ending. They said that there was something wrong with me, in every situation, and I was the horrible one. They quickly went around talking to others, to build up their "case" against me, to somehow make themselves look and feel better. Sadly I lost other friendships because of it. I discovered the other friends who judged me based on conversations that I wasn't included in, were friends after all. My circle of friends became very small at that point, but it allowed me time to heal and love myself.

In being someone with the mentality that everyone must like me, it became very painful having relationships ending that way. But I quickly realized it was their own issues they needed to deal with and I was glad to wake up being me.

> **"Blessed are those who mourn, for they will be comforted." ~Matthew 5:4**

Prayer: *God thank you for putting a shield of protection around me. You heard my prayers of sorrow as my life began to change. I did not know it at the time, but you were creating healthier love and friendships.*

~Amen~

Chapter Six
MY BEAUTIFUL SON

Having my first child, quickly turned things around for me. After ten years of marriage, my beautiful son was finally here. He was absolutely perfect in every way. He slept well, ate well and my life had forever changed. I started growing into the person God had designed me to be. I wanted to be a great mom for him. After all, my dream growing up was to be a mom and a wife. I wanted to be the best at both.

We left the hospital to be greeted by a limousine that his dad had surprised us with. It was so fitting for how I was feeling about finally being a mama. Everything was going to be better now I thought.

But becoming a mom, and "Prince Charming" seeing me as a mom, only created worse behaviors and worse abuse. His relationship with his mom had created even more negative feelings towards me as a mom, because of his unresolved issues with his own mom.

My little boy saw things that no child should see. It was something I never imagined that we would have to live through.

Things got so bad, that I realized that I would need to end my marriage and become a single mom. Because I didn't want my son to be without his dad, I settled with my son being with each of his parents, every other week. My week with him was so great and things were settling in great for my son and I. And then I would be facing the next week without him. It was so painful to have him away from me. I would come home from work and just throw myself on the couch and cry. I felt so heartbroken to not have him with me every day. It finally became so unbearable, that I got back with his dad, and remarried him. I had waited so long for this perfect little son of mine, who I would grow more to love as each day passed.

He has become a man of Christ. He loves and protects his own beautiful family, by learning and growing as a spiritual leader, not only of his family, but with people around him. I watch as he shows his wife and kids respect, kindness and a strong love for God. He is a world changer, and I am so very proud of him.

> **"God is our refuge and strength, an ever-present help in trouble." ~Psalms 46:1**

Prayer: *God thank you for answering my prayers of blessing me with a child. Thank you for reminding me that he is your child who is destined to do great things to honor you.*

~Amen~

Chapter Seven
MY SUNSHINE

The birth of my second child was an absolute learning experience. My beautiful, golden-haired baby girl. My firstborn had a disposition just like mine, so it was easy for me to relate to him. I struggled with my second when she was a baby, thinking she was a difficult child. God opened my eyes to her uniqueness and showed me how to embrace her amazing qualities. This little girl took on the world full speed ahead, in a totally different direction than I would have ever gone. I have learned so much from her. She is an incredible leader in life, who loves, protects and shows such empathy towards others. Especially towards her mama.

As she was growing up, I told her that with good boundaries in her life, she could rule the world with the type of personality she had. She was strong and very assertive and knew how to take life and meet it head-on, with very little fear.

Even as a little girl, she had a way of doing things her way, and it was a great way. Without good boundaries in place, life's adventure could be a disaster for her. She has chosen good boundaries and is such an amazing young lady, making a difference in the lives she touches.

Unfortunately, her strong demeanor created problems very quickly in her relationship with her dad. She wasn't afraid of his bullying and very quickly learned to defend herself and me. This created a lot of pain for her, though. She was quickly and constantly punished. Every time I left her with her dad, I would come home to her in a corner crying, grounded, or in her room crying her eyes out. There was never any validation given for her feelings, and everything was her fault. She refused to cave in to allowing this from him, and she quickly became the most abused in our home.

He was very cruel and an expert at finding ways to break her down. He once watched her fall down the stairs carrying a large instrument she had asked him to help her carry out. She had headed out the door for a recital and slipped down the outdoor steps and fell. She was already hurt and angry at him, and he added to her anger by bursting into laughter. He was a master at bullying people, and those closest to him received his best work.

If she stood up for herself in unfair situations, he would either punish her or bully her to a point she would begin to yell at him through tears, with his laughter to follow. Of course, because of the anger and disrespect she had shown to her dad, she would also be punished.

By the time her spirit was completely broken, and she couldn't take one more day of living with him, she looked up at me and said, "If you don't leave him, I will"! This very strong young lady was once again standing up and wiping herself off. She wasn't going to let the bullying keep her down.

Instead of taking responsibility for his family leaving, he quickly blamed my little girl. He told her that she had said she wished he and I were not married. "Be careful what you wish for", he told her. She was a very strong and smart child who knew who was really at fault for the marriage dissolving. But I do know that the words still hurt her little brave heart. They were very unfair.

I drew strength from who she was, and who she is today. She is one of my heroes.

> **"Do not provoke your children to anger, but bring them up in the training and instruction of the Lord."**
> **~Ephesians 6:4**

Prayer: *God, thank you for bringing this ray of sunshine into my life. I learned through her that I should speak up and stay strong through adversity.*

~Amen~

Chapter Eight
MY MIRACLE BABY

By the time I had lost all hope of ever having a happy marriage, I unexpectedly became pregnant with our third child. After a very difficult pregnancy, my miracle baby was born. My tiny little miracle came into this world on her own terms. God had a plan, and I quickly drew close to Him for guidance in every step I took, being the mom of such a special little girl.

She was born premature, and the miracles quickly began to appear. Most babies born as early as she was spend time in the NICU. She did not have to spend any time there. Our prayers were answered through this first miracle. I am pretty certain that my mom was staying on her knees praying, throughout this time. My babydoll also had not yet developed the ability to suckle, so she was not ready to be nursed or even bottle fed. She was having to be fed through a cup. She was eating very little, and I was getting ready to take her home, with no success in nursing her. I prayed that God would give us another miracle.

The first attempt to nurse her at home, she quickly responded, and another blessing from a desperate prayer was answered.

I spent most nights with little to no sleep. My little girl could not be comforted to sleep. There was no laying her flat or swaddling her for comfort. She would cry out if I did try to lay her down. I had a baby swing next to me that I propped her up in and rocked her all night long. I knew deep down inside there was something very wrong. It couldn't just be that she was born early. Something was wrong. I quickly prayed, "Please God, help me with this baby girl. Please let me keep her".

After three days and nights with very little sleep, as a new mommy who also needed rest, I was sent an earthly angel. My son, who was still very young, walked into the living room on the third night and came to my rescue. He took his little sister out of my arms and told me to go get some rest. It was a school night, and I knew he was very tired, but I went and slept for a couple of hours. What a wonderful gift from such a young child. He was such a sweet and caring son, and still is to this day.

The baby rules that applied with my other two children quickly went out the window. I did not know how to comfort this child, and it was becoming more and more apparent to me that something was just not right.

I went to "Prince Charming" with my fears about my little girl; he quickly quieted my concerns by dismissing them. This was going to become a common theme throughout her illness.

By the time she was nine months old, on her sister's eighth birthday, it became a day that I will never forget. On this day my life turned toward the realization that this was not going to be the journey every parent prays for, but one that God was in total control of. God was sharing His child with me and was already using her for a higher purpose. Something was truly wrong with my little girl. Only God and I knew it at this point.

Her eye was becoming infected. I quickly assumed it was like any other eye infection and called in for eye drops for pink eye. When I put the eye drops in her eyes, she screamed out in pain. It seemed torturous every time I did it, and it in fact was.

The infection became worse, so I took her in to see her pediatrician. He quickly had her admitted to the hospital for a severe eye infection.

My heart ached to be walking into a different world with this new baby. An IV was put into her tiny little hand, and it was just the beginning of a world of IVs and constant blood draws for this baby girl.

After unsuccessful attempts by her pediatrician to clear up the infection through IV antibiotics, he called in an infection specialist. Little did I know he would play a key role a few months down the road in saving my baby's life. The Specialist was not sure why the antibiotics did not work on this little girl, but shot steroids up her nose to clear the infection, and we were sent home.

Just a couple of months passed, and she once again had the doctors baffled. I took her in for severe blisters in her diaper area. I was given antibiotics for her, once again. The antibiotics did not clear up the blisters, but created loose stool, and I had to clean the open blisters with a baby screaming in pain, as I wept with her. A simple task of changing her diapers was truly causing her excruciating pain.

Her flesh was being eaten by the blisters that had become infected. She was running a high fever, and I was alone dealing with this sick little baby doll. I kept taking her to see different doctors, who would refer me to other doctors, not knowing how to treat this child.

I prayed, "Dear God, please help me with her. I don't know how to keep this baby from all this horrible pain." I couldn't bear one more day of watching her suffer such pain. She would soil her diaper, and it would make her scream out in pain as it touched the open flesh.

After several doctor visits, we were once again referred to the infection specialist, who had blood tests run on her. I watched again this little baby doll, having to endure more pain as she was held down for lab draws.

On a Sunday morning, I received a phone call that would not only change my life, but many lives. As I listened, not fully understanding all the medical terms I was hearing, I did hear the words, "Bone Marrow Transplant", and dropped the phone. I couldn't bear to hear anymore.

Yet with this new information and diagnosis, I realized that another miracle had transpired. The disease she was diagnosed with was so rare that the specialist had informed me that he didn't know why he ran the test, but by chance did decide to do so. I am sure God was looking over his shoulder. He was stunned to find out that this little girl had a disease that only two hundred other people in the world had ever had.

My baby girl was diagnosed with an exceptionally rare immune deficiency. She was born with white blood cells that did not have the adhesion (arms and legs) to go down the bloodstream to fight infections. The white cells would multiply, like they did in normal human beings fighting infection, but they would not be able to go down the bloodstream to the infected area to fight the infection. Her deficiency was so severe that she had a one percent chance of survival without a transplant.

With less than 200 known deficiencies, we were quickly referred to another specialist in Salt Lake City, Utah. This doctor was very skeptical of her having the deficiency. She did not have all the common symptoms of this disease, and it was usually diagnosed quickly after birth.

He ran his tests and was very impressed with her original doctor's own testing. He agreed that she did in fact have this rare disease and confirmed that she would be needing to have a transplant in order to have any chance at survival.

He informed us that the next steps we would be taking would be in finding a bone marrow donor who matched her blood type. The best rate in surviving a transplant would be in finding her an identical match. A sibling identical match would create her best chance of a successful transplant.

We were told that the doctor's previous patient had died at the age of five, waiting for a donor. We went down with her two older siblings to all have our blood drawn in hopes of finding a match within her family.

I watched as my son bravely had his blood drawn. When it was my little eight-year-old girl's turn, she was so afraid and cried through the process. I quickly stepped aside and asked God to please bless us with another miracle of a sibling match. "God, please let the match be her brother." I realized it would be very tough on my little eight-year-old daughter if she was in fact the sibling donor.

We flew back home and awaited the results. I was very angry at God by this point. I turned to my Pastor about my anger. He quickly assured me that it was okay to be angry. "God can handle your anger Diana, just make sure you do not turn your back on Him." These were words I quickly embraced and held very close to throughout the next chapter of my life.

A few days passed as I received a phone call with yet another miracle. This was not a small miracle, but one that reminded me that God is with me, and my baby girl is His child first, that I have been honored to share with Him. The voice on the other end gave me a true answer to prayers. I was told that she had a bone marrow donor match. It was, in fact, her brother. He was not only a match, but an identical match. The match was one that was usually only seen in identical twins. Thank you, Lord Jesus, for my baby's chance at life.

I knew with that information that God had a special plan for this little girl. He showed me every step of the way that she was on a special journey.

> **"For with God nothing shall be impossible."** ~ Luke 1:37

Prayer: *God, thank you for growing my faith through this young child. She is a testament to your goodness and grace in our lives. The miracles in her story have been abundant.*

~Amen~

Chapter Nine
LOS ANGELES BOUND

Because my baby's disease was so rare, many doctors with different theories on the type of transplant she should receive,to conquer this rare disease. Hopefully the one we chose would save her life. I remember becoming so overwhelmed by it all. A decision was going to need to be made in choosing the right transplant to save her life. Little did I know, it was going to be one of many life saving decisions.

Again, I needed God to guide me. I was so lost and overwhelmed. I prayed, "God, please show us the direction we need to take for this baby." Later that day after praying, I was speaking to my dad and updating him on all the overwhelming decisions we would need to be making. God spoke through my dad that day, and it would be another step towards saving her life.

I was explaining to my dad about how there were five doctors insisting we needed one type of transplant. Yet one doctor in LA who had been highly recommended by the Specialist that diagnosed her was insisting that a full-blown transplant would need to take place in order for it to be successful. My dad's words came back to me. Those words completely brought me peace in choosing the right doctor. "Diana, just because five doctors are telling you one thing, it doesn't mean that the one doctor standing alone isn't the right doctor to choose". I knew right then and there, we would be heading to the Children's Hospital for a full blown bone marrow transplant.

Once the decision was made, we were told the entire transplant floor was full, and we would need to be placed on a waiting list. It could be weeks, even months before they had room for my little girl on the floor.

The longer we waited, the riskier it would be to keep our baby healthy.

> **"Trust in the Lord with all your heart and He shall direct your paths." ~Proverbs 3:5-6**

Prayer: *God, you have taught me so much throughout my child's sickness, to walk in faith and keep my eyes on you for guidance. Thank you for the many miracles and for using this baby for a higher purpose.*

~Amen~

Chapter Ten
MY SON WAS OFF TO HOLLYWOOD

Before my baby had even been diagnosed, my son had made plans to stay with his cousin for a few weeks during the summer in Los Angeles. He had wanted to pursue his dream of acting and singing. He is very gifted, and we embraced this opportunity for him to go and spend some time in Los Angeles. Little did I know that we would quickly be following him.

My sweet baby girl was diagnosed a week before her first birthday with her rare blood disease. I made sure her first birthday was one for all of us to remember, not knowing if she would ever celebrate another one. Within a few weeks of that special celebration, we were flying "off to Hollywood". Those words took on an entirely different meaning for me.

> **"Be strong and courageous, for the Lord your God is with you wherever you go." ~Jerimiah 29:11**

Prayer: *God, thank you for guiding us and changing our direction when there is a higher purpose for our lives. You have been guiding our steps and leading us towards a bigger and better tomorro**w.

~Amen~

Chapter Eleven
CHILDREN'S HOSPITAL

The wait for a bed was much shorter than anticipated, and we were quickly off to California.

I handed over my baby girl to the nurse, not knowing if I would ever get to take her back home again. As the day went on and the information was processed, I realized just what a miracle it would be to get to take her home again.

As a very attentive little student, I made sure I read through ALL the information that was given to me. One item that was handed to me was pages upon pages of side effects from having a bone marrow transplant. I read every word on every page. I dropped the book and wept.

Though the miracles continued, I became very discouraged and fearful of what lay ahead. I realized, though we had been through the trenches, it was only the beginning of the battle to keep this little girl alive. Many years of life and death decisions that I would have to make, through God's guidance.

The transplant floor was full, and viewing babies up on the floor was very discouraging and alarming. We learned that one of the babies had been on the floor for over three years. Between unsuccessful transplants and complications, this child's life had been only knowing a hospital room. The more I learned and witnessed, the deeper the pain inside was growing.

Our new home was the Los Angeles Ronald McDonald House. I would leave my little girl in the care of the wonderful nurses, as I slowly walked back to my new home to take care of my other two children. This was all so overwhelming. How could this be happening? This little family is surrounded by strangers. Families all going through similar heartbreaking situations with a little one.

I continued to put on a smile as I held back tears. I was cooking dinner while sharing a kitchen with many other families. I really just wanted to be alone. I was scared, angry, confused, and most of all, wanting to close my eyes, only to open them again, waking up from this horrible nightmare.

I was walking toward the kitchen, and someone grabbed my hand. It was "Prince Charming", actually being just that. He pulled me into a quiet room and told me it was okay to cry. I stood there in his arms and wept. I will never forget that kind gesture from him. It was one of the few rare moments where he acknowledged my pain. I realized that when things were really difficult, if he acknowledged how painful it was, he would have to deal with the pain. He usually chose not to deal with it, but to bury it.

I later saw his pain and fear come out in the form of anger toward the rest of us. If we choose not to deal with our emotions, they will eventually come out in some form. His form, sadly, was anger.

My pain was shoved down so deep inside, I eventually started to shut down. Completely.

I grew close to the families both at the Ronald McDonald House and Children's Hospital. We all became like family, as we rallied around one another in support.

At the hospital, I had a habit of going and checking in through the windows of each family. Offering my love and support through the glass windows that isolated and protected these fragile children from the outside world of germs and viruses. Their immune systems had been wiped out through the transplants, and every precaution was taken to protect their precious bodies that could not even fight a common cold without endangering their lives. They lived in their own isolated rooms, fighting for their lives.

I had also become close with the nurses. Some days, as I took a quick tally of how things had gone throughout the night before, I knew by the looks on their brave faces and loving smiles if things on the floor were about to go horribly wrong. I could see it in their eyes. I knew that one of their little ones was not going to make it, and they were preparing themselves to once again say goodbye. The nurses watched as the families grieved in realization that their greatest fear was coming true. It was not in fact a bad dream, but a horrible reality. They had only days, or even just a few hours left with their little one.

I saw doctors running toward the doors and knew they were headed down to the NICU to say goodbye to one of their children they had fought so hard to keep alive through their amazing love and wisdom. I prayed in my heart it would never be my little girl they were running to see one last time.

One day a new family came on the floor. I watched while playing with my baby girl. She had become known as the little princess on the floor. She was the only baby girl in the transplant unit and had her princess wave down. Making sure she waved to anyone who stopped to say hi. I knew the fear this new family had in their hearts. I had just been there. They would constantly come and watch my busy, little, happy baby, and I knew it was to draw hope from her. I also knew it was what kept them strong, to get through the unknown.

I would come in and stop and say hello through the glass window, in hopes of offering some comfort and support. One day, I stopped and noticed that things had changed. The mommy was holding her naked little baby boy in her arms. She looked up at me through her masked face, and I saw it in her eyes that she was saying goodbye. I buried my tears as I offered my love through the window. Putting on a smile, I went in to hold my own little girl. I had to leave the pain and the fear outside her door. She needed her mommy to believe and stay strong.

> "Do not fear, for I am with you. I will strengthen you and help you." ~Isaiah 41:10

Prayer: *God thank you for being my strength and carrying me, through a time that I had no strength of my own.*

~Amen~

Chapter Twelve
IS THERE A PILL FOR HEARTACHE?

One day I walked into my baby girl's room and noticed that something was terribly wrong. I could see it in her nurse's eyes. I watched for some time and tried to read the mood on the floor by watching the nurses I had grown close to. We had all grown close enough for me to quickly realize that something was wrong. Something to do with my little princess.

Oh no, what was it? What has gone wrong? We had already been told that her transplant was a success and that we could take this baby back to the Ronald McDonald House in a few days. How could there be something wrong?

I quickly pulled off my hospital attire and walked to the nurses' station. In a quiet voice, I told one of my baby's nurses that if she did not tell me what was going on, I would pull her ponytail until she did. She knew that I would not let it go, so she pulled me aside to inform me that some lab work had come back, and my baby's old blood cells were taking over her brother's transplant cells, and that there would need to be a second transplant. The first transplant was unsuccessful.

I thanked her for telling me what she had shared with me and assured her that I would not let anyone know that she had said anything. Within moments, I was informed that the doctors would like to have a conference with us. I left the floor and had my few moments of grieving and pulled myself together for the meeting. I already knew what was about to be said. It helped me to stay strong. In my eyes, I felt after all they were doing everything they could to save my baby's life.

This staff had fought hard to take care of a little girl whose disease was the first one of its kind on that transplant floor. I know it was a lot for the hospital staff to take on. I knew they had done their best. But unfortunately it wasn't enough to be a successful transplant. And my baby girl's battle was far from over.

> **"The God of all comfort comforts us in all troubles." ~2 Corinthians 1:3-4**

Prayer: *God, when I didn't think I could take another step, you gave me the strength and courage.*

~Amen~

Chapter Thirteen
SECOND TRANSPLANT

The second transplant would bring on more possible side effects, with a lesser chance of survival. We had to start over, with much less hope than before. While continuing to watch other children lose their battles, we had to hold on to hope. All we could take was one day at a time, sometimes moment by moment.

While all this was going on inside the hospital walls, I would leave knowing that other families that lived with us at the Ronald McDonald House also had their daily battles. Day after day, as I grew to know these families, I could tell when the battle at the hospital had turned grim. I could see the anguish in their eyes as they continued to move on as though things were still okay. This took all they had, but they loved their child enough to stay strong and keep the pain and fear of what was soon to come away from this child who had already been through so much. There was no more hope, and they would be returning home to their far away State, or in many cases Country, to draw close to family and friends as their child slips away. Hope was gone, and no words could be offered to take any of their pain and sorrow away.

I knew that our recent news was painful, but I drew strength in knowing we still had hope, while some families did not.

My healthy children lived with us at the Ronald McDonald House for almost an entire year. They watched as the children they were playing with one day were gone the next day.

After the second transplant, we were eventually able to bring our miracle baby over to be with us at the Ronald McDonald House. I was overjoyed the day that I finally got to take her off that transplant floor!

One tough day, things changed and my baby girl had to be readmitted to Children's Hospital for complications due to cell rejection. We did not know how long we would be living at the Ronald McDonald House, and the lifestyle was wearing on us all.

Family and friends back in Idaho offered to watch over our two oldest children so that they could go back home and continue on with their lives. I would miss them dearly, but knew I was not able to physically or mentally be there for them. They needed to be back in the normal world. To go back to school and be around family and friends.

Within a couple of months, we too were able to take our little girl back home to Idaho. It was going to be a big responsibility to keep up on all her medications and watch for any signs of illness that could harm her, or even take her life. She would be in isolation in our home for the first few years after we returned home with her.

> **"When my heart is overwhelmed, lead me to the rock that is higher than I." ~Psalms 61:1-2**

Prayer: *God, thank you for choosing me to take care of this miracle baby. I am blessed that you have shared her with me, to tell her "God Story" and lead others to Christ through her incredible testimony of miracles and healing.*

~Amen~

Chapter Fourteen
BACK TO IDAHO

During this time in my youngest child's life, she was very sick and needed my care twenty-four hours a day. With her disease being so rare, there were times that her treatment was done day by day, in hopes that she would respond to it.

I hesitated and even postponed writing about this part of my journey with her because it was truly the scariest and most painful part of my life.

I struggled to keep writing, just because I have buried so much of the pain deep down inside.

But I know her journey and the many miracles that God has blessed us with throughout her sweet life, has actually saved a soul.

I had a dear friend who was closely following my baby's carepage share with me that she did not believe in God until she saw Him working through my baby.

This friend has such a precious spirit, and is now saved. That is ultimately why we are here on earth, and I am grateful that God has used us all to bring people closer to Him

> **"The sufferings of this present time are not worth comparing with the glory that will be revealed." ~Romans 8:18**

Prayer: *God, please help us through the valleys. Lord, that we continue to glorify you and remember that we are your children. We are here for a higher purpose. Our stories are not our own, but yours, as your children.*

~Amen~

Chapter Fifteen
IT'S TIME TO FINALLY WALK AWAY

As life went on, we hit some financial stress. As the stress continued, the kids' dad became more and more aggressive. Once again the physical and emotional abuse came at a fast-paced cycle. But sadly, this time, our children were a part of that cycle.

I didn't know how to leave. But my daughter quickly made arrangements for herself to spend her spring break with her cousin, out of our home. I knew it was time for me to step out on faith and leave this brutality once and for all.

At least I thought at the time leaving the brutality was once and for all, but quickly realized, with three shared children between us, the brutality was going to continue at any opportunity he was given. I thought I would be free of the anger and abuse, but I was wrong.

I turned to God and asked Him to take care of the girls and I, as I began to pack up our things, not knowing what the future would hold for us.

Unfortunately, my oldest, my son, was away from the home most of the time and saw very little of what was really going on. Several times the girls and I slept together in the living room, in fear of their dad. We also locked ourselves in the bedroom until we felt it was "safe" to come back out. My oldest daughter and I were so broken and angry by this time, and what my son was seeing was our anger.

His dad quickly turned himself into a victim of our anger and told my son that his sister was a very disobedient child and I was undermining his authority as a parent to discipline her. The problems in our home were quickly blamed on her and I. When I left, I had to leave with my son believing what he was told by his dad, that our marriage was ending because of his sister and I.

It was going to take all I had to keep going, to take care of my little girls. I didn't have the strength or energy to stand up to what was going on between him and his dad. I also didn't want to put my son in the middle, anymore than he was already. The way I saw it, I was certain that through my son's eyes, I had walked away from him and taken his family away. It was truly heartbreaking.

> "I will give you a new heart and put a new spirit within you." ~Ezekiel 36:26

Prayer: *God, please soften our hardened hearts and mend our wounds. Please help us to see people through your eyes and strengthen us through love and grace towards one another.*

~Amen~

Chapter Sixteen
MOVING THROUGH THE PAINFUL PAST

God wants us to love ALL, especially those that are hardest to love. I do know only God can heal angry hearts. I continued to pray and have hope that someday this man would not be allowed to create constant pain and grief in our lives.

In my mind, God is teaching me to stay peaceful regardless of what is going on in the world. I must trust him in every situation, and by doing so, try to stay peaceful through the storms in my life. Even the ones that hit closest to home.

We have choices in life. As adults, we know right from wrong, regardless of what happened in our past. There are amazing and helpful support groups and therapists that can give us the tools in life to cope with our pasts and go forward in living a healthy, happy life, regardless of what has happened in our past.

It is not easy to relearn beliefs and behaviors, but with hope and faith, we can do anything. God will guide us forward, and all we have to do is turn to him for guidance and allow him to work in our lives. If we work through our struggles, we can teach others how to do the same. If we quit in life, the enemy wins. Why not refuse to lose!

I have been through intense therapy and six weeks of classes to learn how to cope with working through the pain, instead of shutting down and going away. So now is the time to apply those skills and make them work for me through the rest of my journey here on earth. God is with me. He has taught me to use my God power... it will be okay, Diana. If God can be for us, who can be against us?

Sometimes I do, in fact, just want to stop and shut down. I am a strong woman and I know God has brought me to this point, and will give me strength and knowledge to get through this part of my journey.

The past is just that — the past. As I reflect on my writing, I must remember just that.

Once I was divorced from "Prince Charming", Sybil occasionally would come to my defense. I was unaware of her existence, and just thought it was a confident new me! I would have some mending to do with relationships, as her aggressiveness was, as a friend put it, like a dragon released. After she would slip away again, I was shocked I had behaved so strongly, and would have to apologize for being so harsh.

I was still faced with the never-ending bullying in my life, by Prince Charming. Any chance he saw to create a way to lash out at me, he would. Sadly, a lot of it came through manipulating my kids.

When I was at my lowest, attending six weeks of coping classes after a stay at the hospital on suicide watch, he decided it would be an excellent time to kick me while I was down. As I was lying on my couch, thinking I can't go on anymore, the doorbell rang. I opened the door to find someone there serving me court papers. Prince Charming was suing me for custody of my two girls, because of my "mental issues".

He had privately told my oldest daughter that he needed to save money on child support. Even though neither of them wanted to live with him, he saw an opportunity and took it.

The court date was fast approaching, and since then my youngest child had been pulling away from him, no longer wanting to go over for visitation. She told me she no longer felt safe around him. She had quickly seen through his manipulation, and it backfired on him. This little girl and I have a bond that no one could ever come between. We have been through the battle for survival. She survived a rare blood disease with two bone marrow transplants. I stayed by her side through a battle that she was going through, and she had seen me rise back up from my own battle of surviving PTSD. The way she responded to his manipulation was quickly blamed on me and I was now facing a second court case brought on by him. The prince of contempt of court had pressed charges against me for interfering with his visitation rights. I had watched my little girl hide behind a couch in fear, as he tried to bully me around in forcing her to leave with him.

> **"No weapon formed against you shall prosper." ~Isaiah 54:17**

Prayer: *God, thank you for being our protection throughout the time of confusion and chaos. Thank you for helping us all to heal from our past wounds.*

~Amen~

Chapter Seventeen
THE UPCOMING TRIAL DATE

My attorney had retired before the trial date and offered to have another attorney take his place. As I was praying, God told me to be still and not pursue another attorney. I decided to focus on staying peaceful and letting God fight my battle against their dad. God will deal with him in a way no attorney ever could.

I went to court, never dreaming he could re-trigger me and bring me back to PTSD nightmares. My body could barely move from all the physical pain, and the tears kept flowing. The pain was so deep that I could barely tolerate it. Someone made the comment one day that it is selfish for someone to commit suicide. If they knew what the intense physical and emotional pain felt like, they would have realized that comment was very unfair. Some people believe that is the only way to stop the intense pain. There is nothing else being felt but pain. Not love, not hope, not happiness, but only pain.

Luckily, God showed me that it was not the only answer. I lived a few months in absolute peace. It was the best feeling

I had had in years. I hadn't felt that much peace since I was a child. But I now know that peace and contentment were there because I had very little contact with him and I had moved away. Not far enough away, but away.

I was determined to write more. At times, I was disconnecting and trying to go away again. My mind wanted to shut down. I wanted to get him out of my head. He had hurt me again in court. He was brutal and mean. Once again in our meetings, I wasn't able to speak. He talked over me aggressively, while saying nothing that made sense. Just talking to shut me down.

He let it go all the way to the trial date and then dismissed his case right there, after seeing both my girls walk in to share their testimonies.

The day I got home from court, after having contact with him again, I started struggling. By evening, there was a text coming from him. Even though he promised my youngest daughter at the courthouse that he would not force her to visit him, he hoped that they would be able to spend time together soon. He was once again banging at the door to get her to come with him. She ran and hid at the neighbors', as he once again called the police on me.

I found myself in bed trying to keep my mind from shutting down again. How would I get back on track? I don't remember.

I was so angry that my peace was gone again. I wanted it back. I now knew that I could find that peace again. I had it before and I could have it again. God would get me through this. Ending my life was not the answer to shutting the pain off. My mind was jumbled and it was hard at times to think through things clearly. Sometimes it was difficult to even form a complete sentence. I needed to have complete focus on each move I made some days. My body was weak and there were days that were hard to even hold my head up. Prayer gave me my life back again.

As my therapist once explained, my brain has an engraved pattern toward the survival side. She worked with me in strengthening different brain patterns, but once I was bullied in court again by him, I seemed to be stuck back in the survival pattern.

"He hears the cry of the afflicted." ~Job 34:28

Prayer: *God, there were times when I had no words to pray. But you knew my heart and protected me when I was lost on how I could protect my children. You protected them for me.*

~Amen~

Chapter Eighteen
JESUS TAKE THE WHEEL

One day a strong and painful memory came back. I remember driving down on the interstate, feeling myself starting to slip away. My brain was on overload and was starting to shut down. It happened so quickly, and I wasn't able to pull my car over. I asked God to take the wheel before I faded out.

As I opened my eyes again, I was still going down the freeway at eighty miles an hour and noticed there were tears rolling down my face.

God had actually taken the wheel while I had faded away. I am not really sure why I had mentally shut down, but it was usually because of too much stress and not feeling safe.

> **"The Lord your God is with you wherever you go."**
> **~Joshua 1:9**

Prayer: *God, thank you for placing earthly and heavenly angels of protection around me.*

~Amen~

Chapter Nineteen
GONE FOREVER

Sitting in one of many appointments with my therapist, I was shocked to hear her saying to me, "Diana, I thought you were gone forever."

I had no idea that it was an option to stay safely tucked away in my world of shutting down and mentally going away when I could no longer deal with all the stress and pain that life had dealt me. I did not know that the ones closest to you would be the people who hurt you the most.

How did this happen? How did I get here? Why was I being looked at like I was a crazy person? I was not crazy, but broken from all the pain.

All I wanted as a little girl was to grow up to become a wife and a mommy. I had so much love to give and I couldn't feel any more love. I can only feel the pain.

I needed the pain to go away. The only way I knew how to make it go away was to shut down mentally in order to survive.

I didn't want to be here anymore. I wasn't crazy; I was just no longer able to cope with what was happening around me.

I was numb and could no longer give love or feel love. The pain had become so deep that there was nothing else but pain.

I wasn't shown what healthy love was when I was growing up, and it continued as an adult.

> **"Above all, clothe yourselves with love, which binds everything together in perfect harmony. Let the peace of Christ rule in your hearts." ~Colossians 3:14**

Prayer: *God, teach me what real, godly love looks like. Heal every place where love has been distorted or wounded.*

~Amen~

Chapter Twenty
NO LONGER HANGING ON

I was told by my Pastor that I couldn't leave my marriage. I had a sick child, young children and we were a one income family.

I was a stay at home mom taking care of everyone and everything around me, but myself. We had one family vehicle, and an immune suppressed little girl who was medically unstable.

But I knew I could no longer hang on. I also knew that my pastor didn't know that there was nothing left inside of me that would allow me to keep hanging on.

I also knew how big my God was, and on faith I left our home and asked God to please watch over us, and He did!

As the therapist worked with my brain patterns that had driven a deep pattern of survival mode, it stirred up painful memories that had been buried deep inside and needed to actually come back out and be dealt with.

Dealing with these memories actually caused me extreme emotional and physical pain. Some days it would hurt to even walk. Most of the memories came out in dreams and random thoughts.

I pushed on and refused to allow the pain to keep me from getting out of bed each day.

I knew if I didn't keep moving forward, the depression would get even deeper and I just couldn't handle being any sadder. Tears rolled down my face as I allowed myself to remember what had happened.

I learned how to cope with my painful past, through extensive coping classes. As I put on a smile and sat with a group of people who were also being taught how to get through life's struggles, I was actually grateful to be there.

Once it was realized that even hearing the sound of "Prince Charming's" voice would trigger me to go into survival mode, Sybil appeared to protect me. I would do everything in my power to not hear his voice when he came to pick up the kids for the weekend.

I remember going into the bathroom and turning on the shower with music blaring to make sure I didn't hear the sound of his voice.

If I would have heard him, my sixteen year old self (Sybil), would come out in full armor to protect me from others around me, even though I really didn't need protection. My brain would just slip back into survival mode, if I did hear him. I would be back to having suicidal thoughts and sinking into a deep depression for at least a couple of days.

> **"I lift up my eyes to the mountains. Where does my help come from? It comes from the Lord." ~Psalm 121:1-2**

Prayer: *God, thank you for coming alongside me through all of my journey and guiding my steps. For giving me courage and strength to keep pressing forward.*

~Amen~

Chapter Twenty-One
AN UNEXPECTED MESSAGE

One day I was sitting by myself in church, holding back my tears, as I had learned to do so well. My goal in sitting there was for His words to heal my pain and give me the strength to hold on. Little did I know that the words I was about to hear would be life changing and actually save my life.

My pastor was in the middle of his sermon when he stopped and closed his Bible. He said he had a message placed on his heart. Even though I am sure it helped many in that congregation that morning, in my mind it was actually a message sent to me directly from God, to help me move in the right direction.

Strength came to me as I was listening to every single word that he was saying. I knew that it was my answer to prayers and gave me the courage to make life saving changes in my life. Not for just me, but for my children as well. Though it might take a while for them to realize that I did it for them as well.

I had held on for so long, too long, because I didn't want my kids to suffer from the pain of divorce and a broken family. But I now realize that I was going to be teaching them healthy boundaries and what healthy relationships look like. There would finally be peace in our home. A home filled with peace, love and serenity. No more strife, insecurity and confusion with absolute chaos. It was time to receive God's peace. And that we did!

It didn't happen immediately though, because I still needed to deal with Sybil. Sybil would need to realize that I would be okay. She didn't need to keep coming out, to defend me. Her sixteen-year-old self was becoming destructive in my other relationships.

That Sunday morning in church, as my pastor closed his bible, he had a message to share. I teared up writing this because of how grateful I am that he was led by the Holy Spirit and allowed the Holy Spirit to interrupt his Sermon to speak to me, through him.

He said, "I want to share something with all of you, but I am mostly directing this to the men in this congregation. I don't care what has happened in your childhood, as grown adults you know right from wrong! You can not keep blaming your childhood as an excuse for wrong behavior as an adult!"

Those very words changed my life! The father of my children had grown up in an abusive home. He suffered dearly from it, and the abused became the abuser.

The more anger he directed towards me, the worse he became.

I always accepted his behavior, because I understood who he was really angry at. I accepted it until I heard these life changing words in church!

YES!! He was an adult, and he knew treating me that way was wrong, but he chose to keep doing it. And I kept forgiving him and allowing it, as I slowly was losing my joy of living, and not putting my own happiness first.

You can understand why someone has bad behavior, but you absolutely should never accept it!

We are all responsible for our own happiness. Keep those healthy boundaries out of love and respect for yourself.

We have only one life to live and the people around us should value who we are!

I sat writing, realizing that staying healthy minded and peaceful while I thought about and wrote about my journey through an abusive past, is a constant process and effort for me to stay in my present life of peace, while I go back to places I'd rather forget.

I had resigned to the fact that I would always have to live with PTSD. But through my own personal growth with God, and lots of prayers, I know I can receive His full healing and restoration by inviting Him to fully heal my wounds.

We can find our peace and joy and be happy again!

"You have not because you ask not. ~James 4:2

Prayer: *Thank you God for teaching me how to lean on you and feel comfort in knowing that you will always be my justice, and right what is wrong.*

~Amen~

Chapter Twenty-Two
GOD'S HAND IN A NEW LIFE

After walking away from my marriage, I asked my family for some pretty big prayers to be sent up. I needed another miracle. I needed a roof over our heads, but couldn't go to work because my youngest had health issues and was immune suppressed.

I boldly asked God for a home of our own, filled with peace.

God had placed it on my heart to pray a big prayer! What the world thought was impossible, was possible through God.

I had reached out to my prayer warriors asking for prayers. I needed God to provide us our next home.

Within two days, my mom had called me about going to look at a townhouse that her friend was going to be renting out while he was living with family, to deal with health issues.

Within a few hours we found ourselves sitting in front of a townhouse, with no answers as to how this single mom was going to be able to move her little family into a home, with no money or job. We all believed God would answer our prayer though!

As we were sitting there, my mom reached out to her friend, asking if it were possible for us to see his home. He was out of town, but said his brother was a block away and could swing by to show us the townhouse.

Everything was quickly unfolding and God had already worked out all the details. We just needed to know and believe that!

We walked into the home, and it was perfect! It had been completely renovated and was more than I could have ever have hoped for. I had to keep everything pretty sterilized, because of my youngest being immune suppressed. I was so thrilled to see that everything was new and clean! There would not have to be hours of scrubbing, before I could even bring her in.

I told his brother, who also had several rentals of his own, that I wanted this home but I didn't have any money in my account for a few more days. He handed me the keys and told me that he trusted me.

The place was now mine! Just like that! It was all God! He opened every door for me, because my mom and I had just enough faith to keep going forward in knowing God would take care of us. Thank you God for answered prayers. Bigger and better than I could have ever imagined!

> **"Whatever you ask for in prayer, believe that you have received it, and it will be yours."** ~Mark 11:24

Prayer: *God, thank you for not only meeting all my needs, but giving me more than I could have ever dreamed of.*

~Amen~

Chapter Twenty-Three
GOD'S MANY MIRACLES

When I had walked away from my marriage, I had left with just the clothes on my back. I didn't even have clothes to wear, let alone furniture or anything else to fill up this new home of ours.

But God knew our needs and brought everything to us.

As we prepared to move into our new home, God showed up in so many ways!

My dad had given me a credit card to use if I needed it. He was always watching out for me. But after seeing all that God was doing to provide for us, I grabbed some scissors and cut up that credit card! I knew God was going to meet all our needs and more!

We had friends and even strangers coming around us to fill up our new home with everything we needed!

One friend called me to tell me that she and her husband had been by the townhouse to drop off a nice couch and love seat for us.

A friend of my brother's had opened a new shop and wanted to send me a beautiful glass-blown dish. When I received the dish, it matched my new living room furniture perfectly!

We watched as our house quickly filled up with the items that we needed. God was placing people around us to send blessing after blessing.

One night I went to bed reflecting on everything that we had been blessed with in such a short amount of time. I closed my eyes to go to sleep and had a thought. Wait! I don't have any silverware! Not thinking about it past that, I quickly fell asleep.

The next day I was with my mom again, and she was introducing me to a friend of hers. She shared all that was going on in my life. In my mind, over sharing, as moms tend to do. (Haha). The gal she was speaking to looked at me, and out of the blue asked me if I needed silverware. Look at God!

I even had a girlfriend offer me an entire bag filled with beautiful clothes! They fit me perfectly!

> **"But when you ask, you must believe and not doubt."**
> **~James 1:6**

Prayer: *God, thank you for teaching me to pray boldly. To not only ask prayerfully, but to believe it will be answered in your perfect timing. ~Amen~*

Chapter Twenty-Four
REACHING MILESTONES

My therapist had a goal set for me. She wanted me to be able to eventually be in the same room with the kids' dad and be okay with it. No triggers, no anxiety, no fading away to my safe place, but staying in my healthy space.

I went from times where hearing his voice would make me mentally disconnect with the world to now being able to have family gatherings. I was able to keep a smile on my face, without a lot of pain behind my smile. But I was actually happy and could feel love and compassion towards him.

I never imagined it was possible, but as I healed, I realized I could actually share the same space with him without losing my peace. Not only for me, but for my kids!

People who don't trust love (and he had every reason not to) need it the most. We can show God's love by how we treat others. I will say, coming to this point was a big journey of healing and growing as a person.

I hear people talk about watching what we even think about towards others, and even ourselves.

When we think negatively about people, they can actually feel that energy.

Having someone around me who resented who I was, because it constantly reminded them of who they weren't, really took its toll on me.

Eventually, the abuse, passive negative comments, shaming, blaming, and whatever else my day held being around him, did eventually dim my light. I started isolating because I no longer wanted to force a smile and pretend everything was okay.

Now I do everything I can to protect my surroundings. People who truly love you will embrace your great qualities and make your light shine even brighter.

"Don't stand on me to make yourself look taller."

That became my motto. If you are trying to step on me, I will place a stronger boundary between us. It's nothing personal; it's just what I deserve.

"You do you, and live how you want to live. I can choose to accept it, or move towards healthier relationships."

I have also realized that any harsh words said towards someone with passive-aggressive behavior will only add fuel to the fire. It would suddenly put myself in a volatile situation, making the situation worse.

I will step back and draw that boundary, yet treat that person with love and kindness. Is it easy? Absolutely not! Is it worth it? Absolutely!

I haven't made the situation worse by trying to defend myself. I have never found myself in a situation where coming up against someone with passive-aggressive behavior will suddenly see the light. They will not admit that they have acted poorly and quickly apologize!. Is it possible? Maybe? But I have yet to see it and would love to hear a positive outcome if anyone has one.

I have really reflected on the people around me who behave like this, and realize, to respond in love is the best way.

I definitely have to step back and deal with my emotions first, so that I can be in a better place to respond. Or not respond at all, depending on the situation!

"Love those who are hardest to love." ~Luke 6:27-36

Prayer: *God, you have shown me to love all. Not only to love those around me, but to love myself. Thank you for teaching me to have Christ-like love.*

~Amen~

Chapter Twenty-Five
THIS TOO SHALL PASS

How true that is! Having faith in those very words has kept me hanging on through the darkest valleys.

I didn't realize that trauma could re-trigger my PTSD, and that I would have to recognize what was going on after a traumatic incident. I have had to learn to ride out the storm and hold on, knowing that what was going on would eventually pass. The loss of hope, the thoughts of suicide were back, but I had the tools to pull me out of survival mode.

God also told me that He can restore me and fully heal me.

In allowing myself to get through to the other side of the trauma, it allowed more growth, strengthened faith and added many blessings that I would have missed out on if I had not recognized what was happening.

I have also learned to work on not staying in my negative emotions. I turned my mind towards all my blessings around me so that the darkness would fade away more quickly.

When my brain was "stuck" in my survival pattern, any triggers would make me feel like I needed to protect myself from everyone around me.

I had to learn how to go from passive to assertive as well. At first, I went from passive to aggressive. The aggressive part of me was the sixteen-year-old "Sybil". Once I felt threatened, she came out to protect me from EVERYONE, especially the person who had triggered me. I would feel that once again love had failed me.

In my mind, I was alone again and that love would fail me. If I had continued down that road of destruction, I would have been the person who sabotaged love, just like my abusers.

I recognized it, but it was a lot of work learning how to assert myself in a healthy way. Sybil was part of me and had to be integrated into my life as someone who accepted that she no longer had to come out to protect me.

> **"To everything there is a season, a time for every purpose under heaven." ~Ecclesiastes 3:1**

Prayer: *God, I was so tired, and you continued to give me hope to know the darkness would not be forever. Thank you for placing people around me to help me through the toughest times.*

~Amen~

Chapter Twenty-Six
FIGHTING THE GOOD FIGHT

Part of learning how to assert myself was intensive therapy. I struggled with antidepressants and all the side effects that came with each new medication. They finally found one that worked, and I was told that I would be on it for the rest of my life.

I was also told by my therapist, as she was trying to make me feel better about being on medication to help my anxiety and depression, that being on medication was like having a couple of cocktails a night.

The next step in my mind was to control my emotions by, in fact, having a couple of cocktails daily.

A year went by, and God placed it on my heart to find peace in Him instead of the alcohol. With the alcohol came weight gain, health issues and relationship issues. I had created a new set of problems!

Not only did God place it on my heart to get rid of the alcohol, but to quit taking the medication that I was told I would be on for the rest of my life.

My psychiatrist had warned me never to try to go off the medication on my own. The dose was so high that it could cause severe withdrawal. Yet God asked me to just stop taking it.

I asked people close to me to pray for me. I didn't know how bad the withdrawals would get, and I was afraid, but knew I would be doing as God asked me to do. So I did it even though I was afraid of the effects.

My family was very concerned, and I faced some opposition. Understandably, but I wasn't going to go against what God had guided me to do.

I knew full well that I could block His blessings if I didn't take His guidance.

I asked them to just pray for me, and I told them that I would be okay.

After a few days of nausea and lightheadedness, I was clear-headed and no longer taking the medication! I hadn't realized how much the medication had been affecting my ability to think clearly!

I came out the other side of this with not only feeling better and thinking more clearly, but with a stronger faith in God! He showed me that I could once again go against what the world thought I should do, but to trust in Him for all my needs.

> **"Fear not, I will strengthen you; I will help you." ~Isaiah 41:10**

Prayer: *God, thank you for showing me that when the world says there is no way, that all things are possible through you.*

~Amen~

Chapter Twenty-Seven
AFTER INTENSE THERAPY

I had put in my work. Therapy was stabilizing me. It was intense, and there was a time throughout it that I had to be admitted to care, not once but twice, in order to keep my promise to not end all the pain myself, but hang on in faith.

I am grateful that I had made a previous promise to my daughter, not to give up and end my life. She saw it in my eyes that I wasn't planning on staying around any longer. She had once again saved my life. That promise is what helped me to hang on and do everything I could to get my life back.

I would have missed out on what God's purpose was for me. I would have never known there would be so much peace and joy in my future.

Luckily, keeping my word is a big part of who I am.

But little did I know that stabilizing my PTSD was just the beginning. As I continued to go forward in life, one day I was driving with my youngest daughter and as I was going through an intersection, someone turned in front of me, as I was driving at full speed, with no time to brake. The violent car accident totaled my car. I was unaware that trauma could re-trigger my PTSD and create a setback. So as I was dealing with severe muscle trauma and a concussion that had my brain so jarred that I couldn't even think straight for several days. I was also left feeling extremely depressed with thoughts of suicide.

My girlfriend had recognized that things were off with me and reached out to a family member about her concerns.

I was quickly seen by my therapist. She explained to me what was going on. I was once again stuck in the survival pattern.

Now, being aware of that, I had received the tools that I could use to work on getting my brain pattern back out of survival pattern and stabilize myself once again.

Tapping therapy technique has always helped me clear my mind and get me back on track again.

Now, with any trauma that I'm faced with, I have learned to recognize when it has affected me to the point that I am dealing with deep depression and suicidal thoughts.

I let people around me know what is happening, and they have been so great at providing me with the love, care, and support that I need in order to work through it.

My boundaries are very solid when it comes to who I let come around me while I work through the trauma.

I intensify my prayer time by starting my morning with a bible plan that is centered around healing, love, peace and faith. Starting my day like this helps me to stay focused on what my thoughts are and helps me to manage my emotions.

> **"After you have suffered for a little while, he will restore you and make you strong." ~1 Peter 5:10**

Prayer: *God, thank you for teaching me how to armour plate myself.*

~Amen~

Chapter Twenty-Eight
ANOTHER NEW BATTLE
TO FIGHT

A study by the American Medical Association found that stress is a factor in 75 percent of all illnesses and diseases that people suffer from today.

As I was sitting with my oncologist, she told me that it made no sense why I was having to deal with breast cancer. It does not run in my family.

I know why I had breast cancer. The stress had taken its toll on me, and it was going to be very important that I started paying attention to my thoughts. I needed to make sure that I left everything in God's hands and quit taking what I'd given to Him back!

There is a lot of healing scripture to dive into when we are sick, as well, and my son spent a lot of time during my cancer battle reading scripture, setting up zoom calls for prayer time, and praise. He would only speak words of life to me.

I am so grateful to have received that kind of love and support from my family and friends. It helped carry me through and once again saved my life.

Not only would my body need to physically heal from all the surgeries and treatment, but I would also need to emotionally heal.

> **"I pray that you will prosper in all things and be in health, just as your soul prospers." ~3 John 1:2**

Prayer: *God, thank you for the messages of healing placed around me throughout my cancer battle. Thank you for all the earthly angels you had around me to love and support me.*

~Amen~

Chapter Twenty-Nine
MORE TRAUMA GIVES ME A CHANCE TO GROW

After my mom's sudden death, I was not only dealing with intense grief but also constant thoughts of suicide. I knew to hold on and what would help me to do just that.

While writing this book, there were days that I found myself having to use the exercises and tools that I had learned in order to find my peace again.

I have found myself in states of agitation, tension, a high heart rate, and tears welling up, almost daily as I was writing.

But this too is an opportunity for me to learn how to remember what I have been through and be able to bring myself back to my peaceful existence. I deserve that, and so do you!

I truly believe God will fully restore me, heal my wounds completely, and there will be a point in my life when PTSD is part of my past.

I realize as I look back on my journey in learning how to win the battle of dealing with PTSD, how grateful I am that I have conquered it throughout those dark days.

If I had not hung on, I don't believe my youngest child would have survived either. Because of so much medical trauma and other traumatic circumstances in her life, she too has had to learn to survive with PTSD. I would not have known how to help and guide her through her darkest days either.

I am grateful that she also has hung on. I have heard her reach out to love and support people who are struggling around her. She is a world-changer and I look forward to watching her fulfill her purpose in life.

I now know because you have held on through your darkest days, you will be able to help others through their valleys, so that they can enjoy the life placed in front of them. A life that can be filled with peace and joy.

> **"God has called me out of darkness into His marvelous light." ~1 Peter 2:9**

Prayer: *God, thank you for teaching me throughout my tough times. Thank you for showing me how to love and support others who are going through their tough times.*

~Amen~

Chapter Thirty
FAITH OVER FEAR

My worrying had gotten to a point that it was affecting my health. I had to strengthen my trust in God, and not just talk the talk but walk the walk.

God had shown me many times that He would meet all my needs. But yet I had developed the habit of worrying with distractions from Satan.

In order not to block His blessings, I needed to grow in my faith and keep remembering to give it all to Him. I would quickly catch that fear that was creeping in and stop myself. At night, when I was tired and it was time to close my eyes and rest, that fear would want to creep in, to steal my peace.

I had decided until I was stronger in my faith, in trusting God to take those worries away, that I would lay my head on my pillow and mentally take each worry I had and picture myself handing each one over to Him, prayerfully.

Eventually I learned to just watch what I was thinking about, and I am still far from perfect at it. But I knew His love for me would cover meeting all my needs and more than I could even possibly imagine!

God showed me that nothing was impossible when I put my trust in Him.

Once I was healed from my past trauma, though there are times I still catch myself slipping back to those painful memories, I realized that I could have compassion for people who struggle with rage and anger. I could pray for them and be grateful that it wasn't me struggling with it. But I also feel if that is something you struggle with, you also need to acknowledge it and deal with it. Deal with it not only for your own personal growth, but for the people around you who get hurt by it. You don't have to do it alone; God will guide you and help you heal.

"If you believe it, you can achieve it!"

We are able to control our own words, thoughts, and actions. If you don't value me enough to control what you say or do to me, I have enough value and love for myself to choose to not accept that behavior from you. It took me years, and a lot of painful experiences, to learn that, but I did!

Live in the moment.

> **"And who of you by worrying can add one hour to his life? So do not worry about tomorrow; for tomorrow will worry about itself." ~Mathew 6:27**

Prayer: *God, thank you for strengthening my trust in you.*

~Amen~

Chapter Thirty-One
PASSIVE AGGRESSIVE BEHAVIOR

My therapist asked me if I knew why I attracted so many relationships with passive-aggressive people. I have had to reflect on that quite a bit.

Most of my, if not all of my, past relationships with men that I dated were in fact passive-aggressive men.

Every single one of them had moms in their lives who had abused their authority over them. It turns out I would be a safe relationship for them. I was a mom they would have liked to have had. I was actually told that by one of them. Because they had not dealt with their painful past, it affected their relationships with other women. They did not trust love, so without even realizing it, they would sabotage it. Once they were comfortable around me, the anger that should have been directed towards their relationship with their moms eventually was directed towards me.

I stayed in relationships too long because of my compassion for what had happened to them. I thought that I could love their pain away. But it was at the cost of my own happiness.

I realized that I was enabling bad behavior for which they needed to be accountable. It cost me my own peace and happiness by staying in the relationship. I needed to have enough self love, to not accept anything less than being treasured and valued. It was time to walk away.

I have also learned not to point out what was wrong with them. It wasn't something they weren't already aware of, and it created more destruction for them to have to heal from. I needed to stay loving and kind, but end the relationship.

I also needed to get out of God's way to let Him deal with them.

I will pray for you. I will stay kind towards you. I will continue to be loving. But I am the daughter of the King of all Kings, and deserve to be loved and cherished.

> **"Therefore, as God's chosen people, clothe yourselves with compassion, kindness, humility, gentleness and patience." ~Colossians 3:12**

Prayer: *Thank you God for teaching me how to love all, even those who are toughest to love.* ~Amen~

Chapter Thirty-Two
EXAMINE YOUR THOUGHTS

My anxiety used to be so bad that it was painful. I just wanted to shut the world out so that I could breathe again. But being a single mom with so many responsibilities, I had to press on. It took everything in me to keep going some days.

I realized that some of it had come from trying to stay strong. So I would hold back tears constantly and eventually forgot how to cry. I did not know that it was possible to forget how to cry, but it is and I still struggle with it today! Crying is healing, so by holding back the tears, it was creating extreme anxiety. I needed to give myself permission to cry again.

I also realized that I needed to pay attention to what I was thinking about. I needed to control my emotions better, and I even realized there were times that I would catch myself holding my breath. Relax. Deep breaths and move forward in peace. Everything would work out.

> "Truly my soul finds rest in God; my salvation comes from Him." ~Psalms 62:1

Prayer: *Heavenly Father, today please don't let me lose my joy, my peace or my focus. In Jesus' name I pray.*

~Amen~

Chapter Thirty-Three
MAKE WHAT'S UNCOMFORTABLE, COMFORTABLE

Living with PTSD, I found myself isolating and not even taking phone calls. When someone would call me, I literally wanted to throw my phone across the room.

Luckily, I refrained from doing that. Phones are expensive after all!

I had learned how to put walls up, and putting my phone on do not disturb was part of that.

I decided to challenge myself in many areas. To start doing what was uncomfortable until it was comfortable.

I may not take the call right away, but I will call back at some point.

I started saying yes to invitations from friends. I also started going on trips, events, and any other invitations that came my way. Previously, I would have excused myself out of most, if not all, invitations!

This life is worth living to the fullest, and I stretched my comfort levels to make sure that I was doing just that!

I sat next to my daughter on a plane and watched her as she had a full-blown panic attack. That was me not too long ago. I have finally learned to get out of my own head and stop thinking about what could go wrong and just enjoy the trip. Sometimes it takes a little more effort because the flight is extra bumpy. But I will do my best to ignore it and to remember that God continues to hold me in His arms. He has given us all His peace, and we need to remember to receive it.

We do not have to keep asking God for His peace. He has already given it to us! We just need to remember to receive it and do our best to keep it.

Satan wants to control our thoughts and take away our peace. We must say, "Not today, Satan!"

"I may not be where I want to be, but thank God that I am not where I used to be."

I am okay and I am on my way!

I will not let anyone tell me that I can not do something, because through Christ all things are possible.

There were people who thought I was gone forever and that I would be on medication for the rest of my life. God showed me that He would heal me.

I was mocked by a therapist for feeling that I needed to write this book. So much so, that it stopped me for several years. My message through writing was tucked away, and I thought it was going to stay there, until God asked me to go forward and share my testimony.

God reminded me that He is with me and that not only was I strong enough to heal from past trauma, but that He will be with me while I write. Guiding me and even teaching me throughout part of this book.

> **"Peace I leave with you; my peace I give you. I do not give as the world gives. Do not let your hearts be troubled and do not be afraid." ~John 14:27**

Prayer: *God, thank you for not only giving me peace, but giving me your peace, as I walk through this chapter of life.*

~Amen~

Chapter Thirty-Four
CHILD LIKE FAITH

Children walk in faith, without the weight of the world on their shoulders to cloud their faith.

We all have had that child-like faith at one time, and our troubles that come to us daily, cloud that truth. Our sadness, disappointments, anger, anxiety, fear, and all the other worldly emotions that distract us from that child-like faith.

We are His children and we can find that child-like faith again.

We can be in this world, but not live like the world.

Another visual that I have had is while I am struggling to keep my peace, I will close my eyes and picture myself in the arms of Jesus. What incredible comfort that brings me.

We are never alone.

> **"Anyone who will not receive the kingdom of God like a little child will never enter it." ~Luke 18:17**

Prayer: *God, thank you for showing me that I am a child of the King of all Kings.*

~Amen~

Chapter Thirty-Five
NOT TODAY SATAN

Satan wants to place fear and doubt in my mind about writing. He is really trying to create that. All that does for me is to want to keep moving forward in sharing my journey with you. If this wasn't a life-changing story, he wouldn't be trying to distract and discourage me from writing by placing fear and doubt in me.

"Not today, Satan!" (Thank you to my youngest child for teaching me that war cry.)

I am grateful for learning to keep pressing on through tough times because of the faith that was instilled in me as a child. Thank you, mom for teaching me about God, and thank you, God, for teaching me daily.

If I hadn't kept pushing through in faith, I would not be here today.

Listening to what the world said, and the lies that Satan wanted me to hear, would have blocked everything that God has been creating me to be. A world changer! He wants that for all of us!

> "Let us not become weary in doing good, for at the proper time we will reap a harvest if we do not give up."
> ~Galatians 6:9 NIV

Prayer: *God, thank you for teaching me not to live like the world lives, but as you would want me to live.*

~Amen~

Chapter Thirty-Six
NEVER GOODBYE, BUT
SEE YOU LATER

When my mom passed away. She was the pillar of our family. Looking back, I realize now that she truly was tired and ready to go.

Because she was such an important part of our lives, we were gifted with God allowing us all to say our goodbyes.

Mom had suffered a major heart attack because of internal bleeding that the doctors were unable to find. She had been life-flighted to the hospital, and the doctor did not expect her to live. But God had a different plan. Her family was spread out across the country and quickly came around her, not knowing why she was in the ICU, and not knowing that this was the beginning of the end. We just knew that she needed us.

We all arrived and quickly learned what had happened. One of my brothers arrived at the hospital and looked at her; she was blue. He thought that it was too late. Again, God is good and has a bigger plan. Within a few hours, we did know that this was a blessing that she was still with us. We quickly discovered that we would be making final plans for her care and would need to say our goodbyes.

She was ready to go, but she held on for an entire month. She hung on because she was worried about her kids not being okay once she left. A caring mom until the very end.

I love you and miss you, Mom. Thank you, God, for the gift of allowing us all to come together and say goodbye. Never goodbye though, but see you later.

With all that being said, my oldest daughter and I realized, without questioning the details or realizing that we were actually going to lose my mom, quickly uprooted our lives and moved back home to Idaho to be around mom. Though we did end up losing her, I was blessed with both my girls moving into a home with me. Another gift from God. I knew that it was temporary, and so did they. We cherished every moment of our time together and thankful for the unexpected blessing of being able to be together while we worked through the grief of losing someone who was so special and loved by us.

Because we were together in the same home, their dad had been in our home a lot and back in my life again. It opened my eyes to what it truly means to love those who are hardest to love. It was easier not to have to think about that when he was not around.

> **"And whenever you stand praying, if you have anything against anyone, forgive him and let it drop, in order that your Father who is in heaven may also forgive you your failings and shortcomings and let them drop." ~Mark 11:25**

Previously, when they were struggling in their relationship with their dad, they would talk to me about it. I quickly became a mama bear and let my own emotions get in the way. I had added negative comments. Is that loving? It is not. In fact, it is damaging and definitely not showing God's love through my actions.

It was going to require a lot of work on my part to change my behavior by letting the past stay in the past. My love for my children and for my Heavenly Father gave me the strength to control what I was saying when they came to me. It was also allowing me to truly heal.

I realized that I should just listen to my kids when they were frustrated. Adding my "two cents" had absolutely no benefit, and was actually getting in God's way of helping them work through their own problems with their dad.

> **"Think on good things." ~Philippians 4:8**

I really had my work cut out for me, and I needed to remember how important it would be to not damage my children's relationships with their dad.

A great way to heal from this past relationship, which I desperately needed to do, not only for myself but for my children, is to think and speak good things about him.

If I am praying for a great relationship between my kids and their dad, then my relationship with him will need to change as well.

As I stayed focused on my thoughts and words towards him, I noticed a sense of peace when I think about him now. I never thought that could ever be possible.

> **"You have not because you ask not." ~James 4:2**

I prayed that God would also heal the father of my children. God requires that our own hearts will need to change before prayers can be answered. We can block blessings when we think and speak wrong.

There was still a lot of work on my part before he could answer that prayer. And I truly believe that prayer will be answered.

I can not pray a big prayer for healing in my relationship with him, or even more importantly my children's relationship with him, if I was causing damage with my actions and words.

Our words can build up or tear down, and it all starts with controlling our thoughts.

Reckless words can cause pain, damage relationships, and lead to regret. Wise and thoughtful words can bring healing and build peace and harmony.

God, I pray for wisdom and thank you for your guidance in fully teaching me how to control my thoughts and words, to be for good. Thank you for helping me to fully heal and to love in a Godly way. For loving me unconditionally and for your grace each and every time that I have fallen short of this.

It will not always come easily for me, but it will become a part of who I am as I focus on changing my thoughts so that my words become words of healing and no longer words that cause damage.

Luke 6:27-28 encourages loving enemies and praying for those who mistreat you.

> **You have heard that it was said, "Love your neighbor and hate your enemy." But I tell you, love your enemies and pray for those who persecute you, that you may be children of your Father in Heaven.** ~Matthew 5:43-45

Prayer: *God, I am grateful for your love that is in me.*

~Amen~

Chapter Thirty-Seven
TO NEW BEGINNINGS

Getting through the trauma is a process worth going through. It allows us to live the lives we are intended to live. So many times I wanted to give up, but I didn't. I still use deep breaths, tapping, praying, going on long walks, prayers from others, big hugs, crying, getting extra rest in or whatever else it takes to get me back to feeling myself again.

I am grateful that I went through EMDR (Eye Movement Desensitization and Reprocessing therapy). It allowed me to process the terrible memories that I had tucked away, trying to forget about them .

It took me out of that trauma and has allowed me to live a joyful and peaceful life that I would have missed out on had I given up.

"Never give up. Today is hard, tomorrow will be worse, but the day after tomorrow will be full of sunshine."

No matter how difficult it is, it is worth getting through it. You deserve the joy and happiness that awaits you.

> **"And let us not grow weary of doing good, for in due season we will reap if we do not give up."**
>
> **~Galatians 6:9**

I was completely checked out and could have chosen to stay tucked away safely in that disconnected place of peace. But I fought to stay connected. In doing so, I had to face and deal with a lot of painful buried memories, along with any other traumatic events that I would still be facing.

Through persistence, I learned to cope with life's challenges in a healthy way so that I could keep living my life in an emotionally healthy way.

I wish I could hold your hand through your dark and painful times. But hopefully, in sharing some of my story, it will be a way for me to help, encourage, and guide you. To encourage you to press on and move towards the peaceful and happiness that lies ahead for you.

We all have a story, and by sharing the details of my years of abuse, I can also share that there is victory that comes from learning how to put our own happiness first. We are all responsible for our own happiness, and trying to make other people happy at the cost of our own happiness is not how we should live our preciously short lives. Let's live our lives to the fullest.

We can find our voices and values. No more compromising! Stand strong in knowing that you love yourself enough not to allow yourself to be mistreated by others.

I have compassion towards people who don't know how to love others well, because you can only love others as much as you love yourself.

I pray that the people who don't value and love themselves will learn how to receive God's love through us.

Don't allow anyone to put your beautiful light out. Keep shining. The world needs your love and light.

> **"For I know the plans I have for you," declares the Lord, "plans to prosper you and not to harm you, plans to give you hope and a future." ~Jeremiah 29:11**

Prayer: *God, thank you for your light that continues to flow through me.*

~Amen~

Chapter Thirty-Eight
I AM AN OPEN BOOK

I used to pride myself on not holding anything back and just being open to anyone and everyone.

Being open to people who do not have your best interests at heart can actually not be a good thing.

It gives those people possible tools to use situations to hurt you.

I had shared my past with someone who I thought I could trust. That person used it against me, to steer away from their own faults. They wanted to make it seem like it was "Sybil" coming back out. I had dealt with that second personality years ago, and only shared my story so that they could know more about me. It wasn't "Sybil" at all! It was the strong, assertive person that I had become, not allowing someone to devalue me and cross strong boundaries that I had put into place.

Thankfully, this stronger woman knew that it was time to put that relationship behind me.

This type of person will try to put your light out, to deflect from their own bad behavior, instead of self-reflection and an apology. More pain has been added to the situation and trust has been broken.

I will pray for you and I will be kind to you, but not everyone gets to be in my inner circle of full transparency.

Instead, I learned that our inner circle has people who embrace our strengths and will not intentionally want to hurt us through their actions and words. None of us are perfect people, and we all can and do things that hurt others at times. But the people closest to us will quickly apologize and will also show us enough grace to accept the apologies as well.

It is a true blessing when we have people around us who will show us healthy love and support us.

I also used to confess to "having a wall up". God taught me that He is my protector, and would always reveal what needs to be revealed in order to protect me.

I don't need that wall up. My Heavenly Father will always be my justice. I don't need to look for things in a relationship that could hurt me. I need to trust that God allows that person to cross my path for a reason, and maybe even just for a season

God will reveal anything that could harm me, and He has every time!

I thank God for those people, because I have learned from every relationship that He has brought into my life.

Self-isolation and a lack of trusting people can truly hold us back!

I pray that while I was in someone's life, if only for a season, that I was a blessing to them during that time. That God's love shines through me and hopefully brings them closer to knowing that there is healthy love out there and that it is worth the effort they need to put in to fully receive and accept not only loving themselves but loving others.

And by all means, trust your instincts! God gave us the Holy Spirit for a reason. If you see a red flag, believe it! I was so good at allowing them to be excused away.

"A red flag, is a red flag, is a red flag!"

"God can do more in one moment than you can do in a lifetime."

We can trust in Him to protect us and reveal what needs to be revealed in all situations.

He will be our justice when we are being treated unfairly. We can keep our peace and rest in Him knowing that He is our protector.

> **"No evil shall befall you. For He shall give His angels charge over you, to keep you in all your ways." ~Psalms 91:10-11**

Prayer: *God, thank you for watching over me when Satan tries to destroy what you have guided me to do and be.*

~Amen~

Chapter Thirty-Nine
LIFE AS A SINGLE MOM

I was struggling at times to get my footing when it came to financial stability as a single mom. I wanted to remain around my young kids, and had my youngest who was immune suppressed. She was constantly sick, and needed me.

It was tough as a single mom to keep an eight to five job, and still provide the nurturing and support that my kids needed from me.

There was a time when my finances were unstable, from moving back to my hometown and starting a new job. I was served court papers and was being sued for custody of my kids, by their father. There were all kinds of allegations that I would need to defend myself against. My divorce attorney had since retired and it was going to cost me thousands of dollars to hire an attorney that would help me defend myself.

While taking it to prayer, God spoke to me and told me to defend myself.

I had realized that every day that I had been searching for someone to help defend me, God was closing those doors.

By constantly praying, the answer came. God showed me through prayer how to file a response back towards the lawsuit. I was being guided on how to represent myself and He protected me every step of the way.

In truth, I had the best attorney I could ask for. The Holy Spirit worked through me.

Not only did the case get dismissed, but his attorney dismissed himself from the case.

> **"No weapon formed against you shall prosper." ~Isaiah 54:17**

Prayer: *God, I have found so much peace in knowing that you are protecting me.*

~Amen~

Chapter Forty
PUTTING MYSELF OUT THERE

Go out there and live your life! Trust that the people who come around you are there for a reason.

Prioritize relationships in your life. Those relationships need to be nourished.

I've started saying yes to going out with family and friends again. Pulling myself out of self-isolation is what blessed me with finally meeting my soulmate.

Self-isolation will not help you strengthen bonds and build relationships in your life. How can we develop and trust love, if we aren't putting ourselves back out there?

I would have missed one of my biggest blessings in life: meeting my husband. Life is precious and we only have one life given to us.

We've got this!

> **"He will cover you with His feathers, and under His wings you will find refuge." ~Psalms 91:4**

Prayer: *God, I am grateful that you are teaching me how to let go and let you take care of me, as your child.*

~Amen~

Chapter Forty-One
FORGIVENESS

I have always known that I needed to quickly forgive in order to move forward, and it is what God wants me to do.

But how do you really forgive from your heart? I was speaking forgiveness, but my heart and emotions still had so many wounds, and kept reopening my hurt and anger.

I also found myself quickly saying, "I forgive you". After all, that is what we are guided to do right?

But I realized that my thoughts towards the people who I had "forgiven" were still negative thoughts and emotions.

I kept taking back that forgiveness.

If we truly want to forgive someone and want to leave the past behind, we need to change our thoughts about that person.

We can act loving and kind towards them, but in order to actually feel genuine love for them, we need to change our thinking first! Changing our negative thoughts about them to positive ones will allow us to be at peace with them, allowing us to move forward from the past hurts.

After all, that is how we want people to treat us after our transgressions towards them, right?

A person's true character is revealed not only by their actions and words but also by what they are thinking about others.

We are not at peace with ourselves or others if our thoughts are not in alignment with our words and actions.

I had thought negatively about certain people who I thought I had forgiven, that it was surprisingly a lot of effort on my part to turn my thinking around.

I decided to take baby steps and just start daily with one positive thought towards that person until I could reach a point where it became less of an effort and more from my heart! It works!

> **"Forgiveness is a divine act of love that mirrors God's mercy." ~Colossians 3:13**

Prayer: *God, please help me to forgive others the way you have forgiven me.*

~Amen~

Chapter Forty-Two
TIME TO SHARE MY STORY

When God guided me to write this book, I had no idea what I was going to write. My mind was completely blank.

I found a journal that my son had given me. That journal had been tucked away, with the pages left blank, for years.

My kids had been telling me for a long time that I should write a book. I would smile and shrug it off, thinking instead that I would prefer to keep my thoughts and memories safely tucked away. That way, this bubble I had created around me, would help me forget that part of my life. But yet, I continued to remind my youngest child that all her painful struggles were for a higher purpose.

Well those were just empty words if I didn't put action into my own journey. Each painfully difficult struggle came with incredible testimony.

If we don't share the victories, we can not help encourage others who are going through similar challenges. It doesn't stay dark forever. Through darkness comes light.

As God brought new people around me, the wall that I had so proudly spoken, stayed around me. I continued to keep people at arms length, so that I could not be hurt anymore. It's truly painful to look back on, but I am so grateful to have learned to trust God, and allow those walls to start coming down. I am still working on it today.

As I moved around for years, with an outer smile and a friendly hello, keeping conversations short, I was also giving off a presence of "please leave me alone, because I won't let you in."

I picked up the journal in faith.

I had no idea what was going to come out. With deep breaths and prayers for guidance, the words started to flow. Some of them even taught me some very powerful lessons because the Holy Spirit had guided my words..

Put the walls down and trust God for His continued protection. How are we going to fully love and serve the people around us if we have those walls up?

Forgiveness, isn't just a word, but an action. We can not fully forgive if we don't deal with those negative thoughts!

What we think about people eventually becomes what we say about people. I am grateful that throughout these pages, I have learned how to truly love and forgive people. This is a new beginning for me, and hopefully for you as well.

God has allowed things to happen in our lives, and will work things out for our good. Keeping our eyes on Him through the tough times will give us the strength and courage to pull through, with a large dose of hope and faith.

We don't always understand why God has called us to do something. But with hope and faith to move in the direction that He guides us, the blessings are abundant.

> **"And we know that for those who love God all things work together for good, for those who are called according to His purpose." ~Romans 8:28**

Prayer: *God, thank you for the valleys in our lives that allow us to learn and grow in our faith.*

~Amen~

Chapter Forty-Three
WE ALL HAVE A STORY

As we grow stronger in our journey from past abuse, learning to love ourselves enough to go forward, we realize that our journey is used for a greater purpose.

Because you have decided to press forward, your journey can help others.

I started writing again, telling my story of my journey with PTSD, feeling very scared. It made me feel vulnerable and fragile. But it came back to me needing to stretch out in doing something very uncomfortable, until it feels comfortable.

Having faith that my story hopefully reaches others to encourage them to get through great challenges in life. To help you realize that you have been chosen to reach out and encourage others as well. You're strong enough to be on this journey, and your story will impact others!

If I don't share and help others, what was this all for?

People have different methods they will use to start writing, to keep writing and whatever comes next.

Mine has become, starting with prayer time, deep breaths and allowing God to guide me and lead me through the process.

It's helped me gain my confidence back in fulfilling my purpose in life.

What is your story? You are valued, and it is important for others to hear your testimony.

You will help others. Even if sharing your testimony helped just one person hang on, it is so worth it!

I started, not wanting to look back at where I was, being reminded of what had happened, and the incredibly dark valley that I had been through. But I wrote just a little each day, in order to keep my brain from getting foggy, my heart to not start racing and my tears from coming back, over memories that I have dealt with and moved on from.

Those first few days of baby steps have brought me to a place of wishing that I could write all day!

Tell your story! You've got this! The world is ready to hear it.

As you do, there are still things to learn about yourself. You are strong, you are valued, and loved unconditionally by God.

> **"For we are his workmanship, created in Christ Jesus for good works, which God prepared beforehand, that we should walk in them." ~Ephesians 2:10**

Prayer: *God, please allow this book to be everything you need it to be to help others learn to love, heal and grow in their faith in you. Thank you for your continued healing of my family. Thank you for your daily grace and love.*

~Amen~